WORLD FAMOUS BUILDINGS

Sagrada Familia

by Alicia Z. Klepeis

BLASTOFF! READERS 3

BELLWETHER MEDIA • MINNEAPOLIS, MN

Blastoff! Readers are carefully developed by literacy experts to build reading stamina and move students toward fluency by combining standards-based content with developmentally appropriate text.

Level 1 provides the most support through repetition of high-frequency words, light text, predictable sentence patterns, and strong visual support.

Level 2 offers early readers a bit more challenge through varied sentences, increased text load, and text-supportive special features.

Level 3 advances early-fluent readers toward fluency through increased text load, less reliance on photos, advancing concepts, longer sentences, and more complex special features.

★ **Blastoff! Universe**

Reading Level

Blastoff! Beginners — Grade K

Blastoff! Readers — Grades 1–3

Blastoff! Discovery — Grade 4

This edition first published in 2026 by Bellwether Media, Inc.

Library of Congress Cataloging-in-Publication Data

LC record for Sagrada Familia available at: https://lccn.loc.gov/2025018583

Editor: Megan Borgert-Spaniol Series Designer: Chase Demmin

Printed in the United States of America, North Mankato, MN.

Table of Contents

What Is the Sagrada Familia?

The Sagrada Familia is a **basilica**. It is in Barcelona, Spain. It towers above the city.

Sagrada Familia is Spanish for "holy family."

History of the Sagrada Familia

The idea for the Sagrada Familia came from Josep Maria Bocabella. He was a **Catholic** bookseller from Barcelona.

artwork of Josep Maria Bocabella

Josep saw a famous church when he visited Italy. He wanted one like it in Barcelona.

Josep raised money to build a church. Workers began building it in 1882.

Architect Antoni Gaudí took the lead the next year.

Antoni Gaudí

Many of Antoni's ideas came from nature. Columns inside the church look like trees.

Some columns were made of **porphyry**. Others were made of dark gray basalt. These stones brought color into the church.

porphyry
column

Antoni added more color with stained glass windows. These windows fill the church with colorful light.

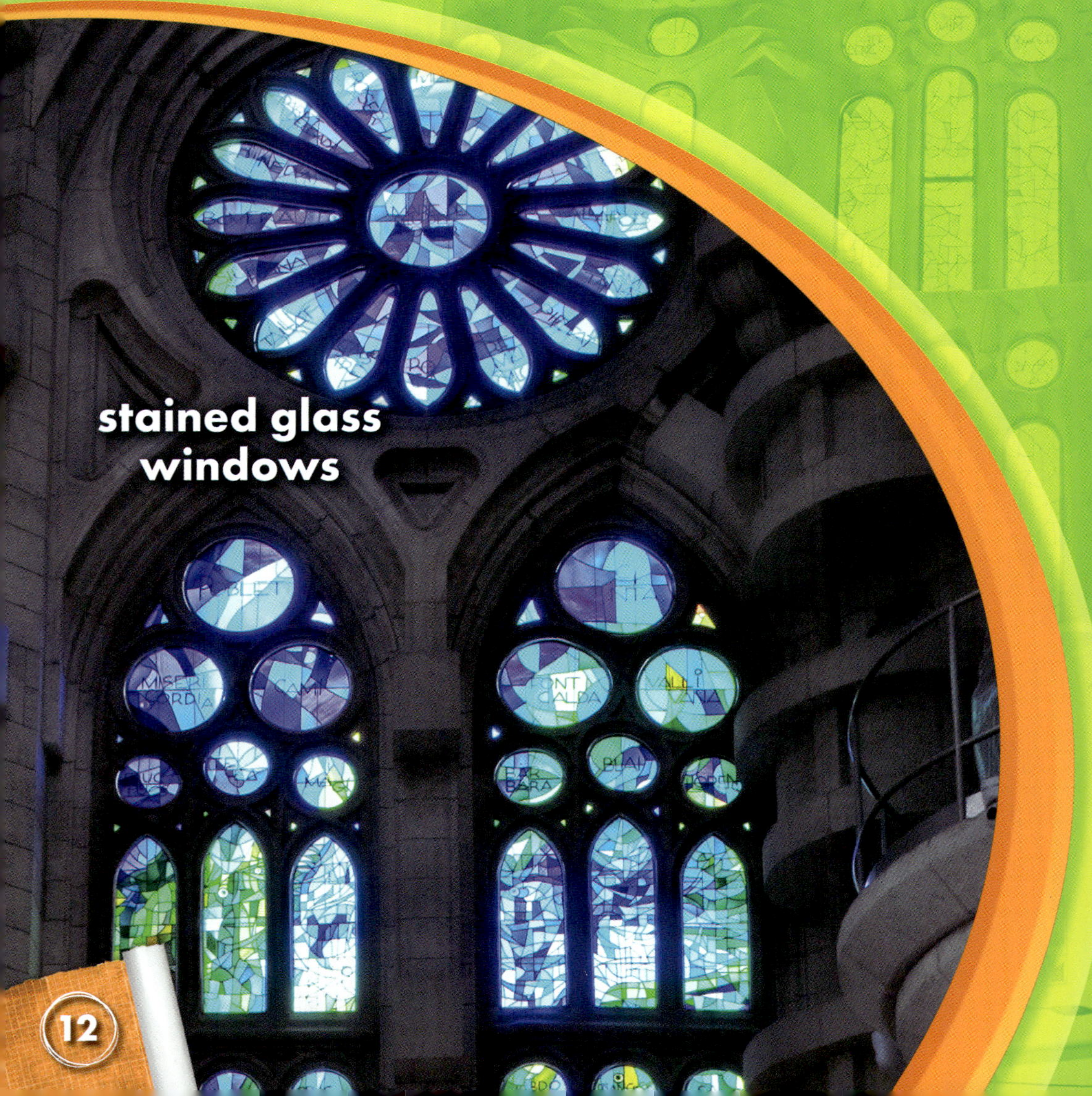

stained glass windows

Building Supplies

Windows on the eastern side are mostly blue. Windows facing west are more orange. Other windows have many colors.

Parts of the Sagrada Familia

The Sagrada Familia is known for its **facades**. They are made up of **sculptures** of people, plants, and animals.

These figures show stories from the life of **Jesus**.

Fantastic Facades

Number of Facades 3

Famous For show stories from the life of Jesus

The Sagrada Familia is 566 feet (172.5 meters) tall. It has 18 towers. The tallest tower honors Jesus.

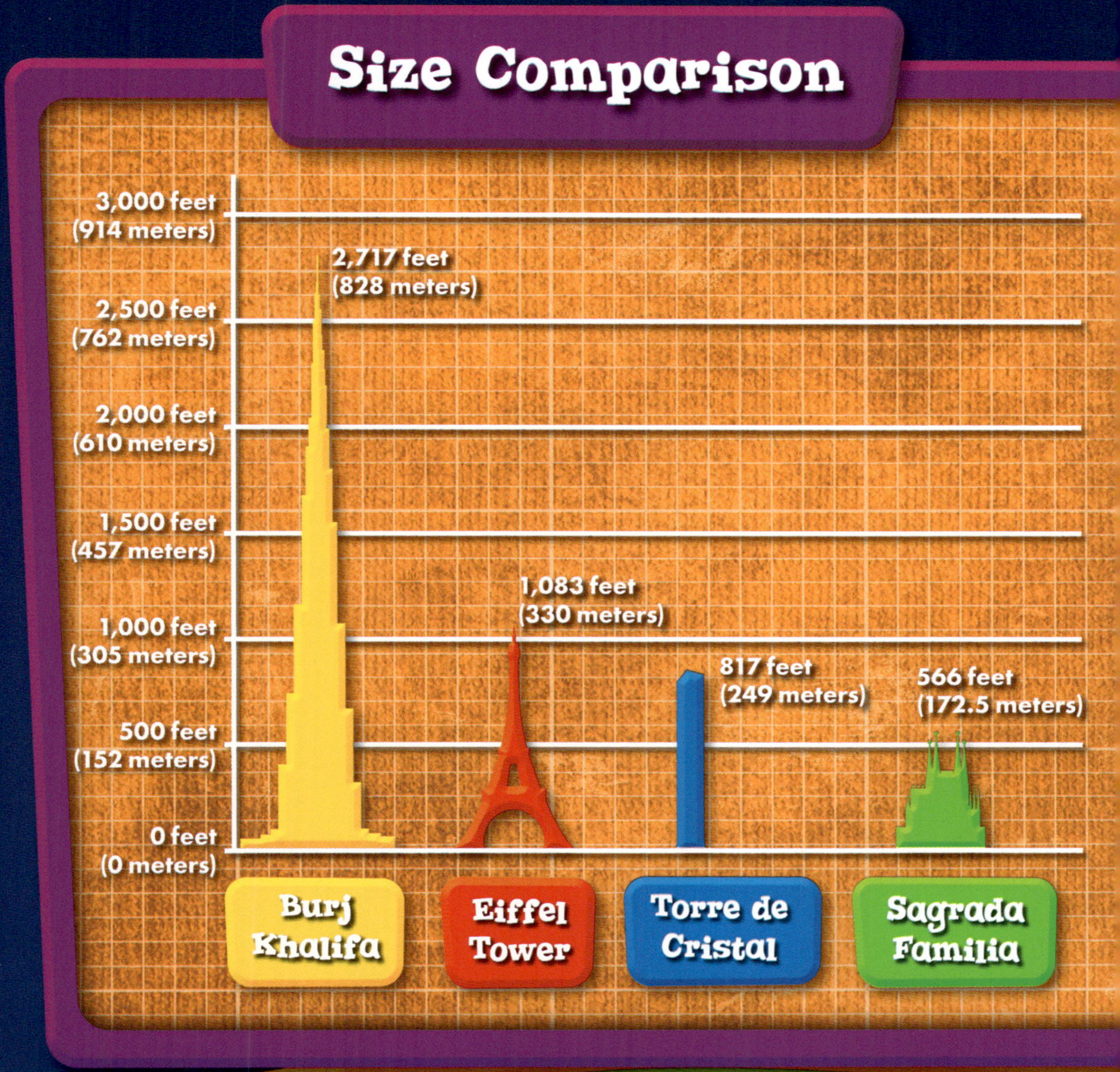

Pinnacles top the towers. **Mosaics** made of glass and tile cover the pinnacles.

The Sagrada Familia Today

Over 4.5 million **tourists** visit the Sagrada Familia each year. It is one of the world's most visited churches.

The church's museum shows early drawings and photos of the church.

Workers have been building the Sagrada Familia for more than 140 years. They plan to finish the main building in 2026.

The Sagrada Familia will be the tallest church in the world!

Glossary

architect–a person who designs and plans buildings

basilica–a church that has been given special honor by the leader of the Roman Catholic Church

Catholic–relating to the Christian church that is led by the pope

facades–the fronts of buildings

Jesus–the teacher and leader who is central to the religion of Christianity; Christians believe Jesus to be the Son of God.

mosaics–decorations made by using small pieces of colored material to make pictures

pinnacles–decorative features that top buildings such as churches and castles

porphyry–a rock containing feldspar crystals set within a dark red or purple base

sculptures–works of art created by shaping hard material into forms

tourists–people who travel to visit another place

To Learn More

AT THE LIBRARY

Anderson, Shannon. *Spain.* Minneapolis, Minn.: Bellwether Media, 2024.

Katz, Susan B. *Gaudí: Architect of Imagination.* Zürich, Switzerland: NorthSouth, 2022.

O'Brien, Louise. *100 Things to Know About Architecture.* London, U.K.: Happy Yak, 2023.

ON THE WEB

FACTSURFER

Factsurfer.com gives you a safe, fun way to find more information.

1. Go to www.factsurfer.com.

2. Enter "Sagrada Familia" into the search box and click 🔍.

3. Select your book cover to see a list of related content.

Index

The images in this book are reproduced through the courtesy of: anek.soowannaphoom, front cover; VD Image Lab, front cover (inset), background (throughout); Sergii Zinko, front cover (inset); Berna Koritan Sonmez, icon (throughout); basiczto, p. 3; NEWTRAVELDREAMS, p. 4; World History Archive/ Alamy Stock Photo, p. 6; Mistervlad, p. 7; PHAS/ Universal Images Group/ Getty Images, p. 8; Gaudi and Barcelona Club/ Wikimedia, p. 9; Tot conflueix/ All's conected/ Wikimedia, p. 10; David Herraez Calzada, pp. 10-11, 13 (porphyry); Mistervlad, p. 12; Albo, p. 13; michal812, p. 13 (basalt); Nadezhda Bolotina, p. 13 (stained glass); Roman Belogorodov, p. 13 (tiles); Cavan, p. 14; shiler_a, p. 15 (inset); Valerie2000, pp. 14-15; Pascal, pp. 16-17; Stefano Politi Markovina, p. 18; Peter Noyce ESP/ Alamy Stock Photo, p. 19; Aerial Film Studio, p. 20; rabbit75_fot, pp. 20-21; Philip Lange, p. 23.